v v v

Shards from the Poet's Mask

v v v

Brian Peter Hodgkinson

Copyright 2023 Brian Peter Hodgkinson

This book is a work of fiction. Names, characters, places, and incidents either are products of the author's imagination or are used fictitiously. Any resemblance to actual events or locals or persons, living or dead, is entirely coincidental.

All rights reserved, including the right of reproduction in whole or in part in any form.

About the Author

Brian Peter Hodgkinson is from Chagrin Falls Ohio. Artistic as a child, won art contests at an early age, graduated from high school and joined the USMC. After the service, was married and fathered four children, two boys and two girls. In his late twenties, felt the call to go overseas as a missionary to Kenya, East Africa and India. Lived and traveled overseas for over twenty years. Returned stateside and attended Hiram College for a degree in the communication field. A grandfather now of seven, he's retired and spends his time writing and traveling.

Foreword

Brian's early life began with sadness and difficulty. Abandoned by a nineteen-year-old mother at age three, Brian spent the next year in an orphanage surrounded by strangers. We were adopted when Brian was four (I, his brother, three) by a loving mother and six-foot-six booming-voiced father, his life creatively unfolded. As a teenager, Brian lived in the art-room at school (cutting classes), and later joined the Marine Corps where his pluck put him in the brig. Then, he found salvation through his belief in Jesus. After an honorable discharge from the Marines, he felt drawn to travel, and for twenty years lived in Kenya, East Africa, bringing encouragement to people while raising four children overseas. Between the covers of this most exceptional collection of Brian's you can find the emotion, pain, successes, mirth, and Brian's point of view. As his brother, we shared a rocky start and I can testify that Brian's poetry shows the road map of an eagle-eyed observant life.

Author's Brother,
Lance R. Hodgkinson

Contents

Tsultrim Dawa 1
The Four Flags Of Easter 3
That's All Folks 4
Freckle Face 5
Hail To the Source 6
Disestablishmentarianism 8
Game of Bones 10
Laugh 11
A Kiss to the Sky 12
Lamplighter 13
Mary Yoders 14
Woodwoses 15
Reflection 16
Enter My Cantillating Den 17
It Really Bites 18
Riding the Canadian at Twelve 20
Turkey Bones 21
Hand Puppets 22
Siri Means Concealed in Swahili 23
Good Spell 24
The Bridge Once Lifted 26
Core Gardening 27
Morte-Saison Gone 28
Mom Dear 30
Workaday Commute 32
Fire Wood 33
A Fiesta 34
Heavy With Children 36
The Lot 37
Flatula-Dracula 38
Lucky Stones 39
Morning Salute 40

The Displacements of War	41
Note to Self	42
Bottomless Cup	43
Morning Stroll With the Cat	44
Feast Before Famine	45
Alghaba	46
haiku #2	47
Rainbow Dorothy	48
Red Lined	49
An Unwanted Visitor	50
Topper	51
Zum-Zum	52
aftermath	53
It Started With One Bag	54
Strutting Her Hightops	55
Woodlore Easter Eggs	56
Underwater Pictures	57
A Tub of Reciprocity	58
eclipse	59
The Reaper	60
The Poet Gripped by a Raven	61
Alfred's Sound Bite; Take One	62
The Sun Swings Itself	63
Traffic	64
The Marina Cat	65
The Gut Punch	66
Stained	68
The Watchman On the Shadowy Decks	69
Vengeance is Mine	70
A Father's Prayer	71
plus-sign	72
Digest	73
No Laughing Matter	75
A Coup Fourré	76
A Beachcomber	77

Out Like a Lamb 78
The Call of Nature 79
[the sun lights day] 80
Lilo 81
Aegis 82
Cat Watching Birds 83
Beyond Spacetime, We 84
Bid a Long Adieu 85
The Grid 86
nothing to give 87
Amber 88
Crossing Over The Equator 90
Have A Look 91
Communication 92
The Optics 94
Watch Care 95
Voyagers 96
Bird Cherry Tree 97
Salts 98
Snap 99
Diamond Girl 100
A Sapphire from Clay 102
haiku #6 10-05-2022 103
De Jure 104
Cat's Eyes 105
Jet Lag Went South 106
Needles 107
Slaked 108
Regatta Afternoon 109
Flash Bulb 110
visiting the - tanka 111
Docking Haiku 112
Green Tongue 113
Sunday Drivers 114
A Nest 115

The Sentry	116
To The Revenant Victor	117
Thought Police	119
Still Smiling	120
Metamorphic	121
To Javelina & to Hold	122
It May Be Love - Dodoitzu	123
Tapestries	124
Bust	125
Play Today!	126
Full of It	127
A Name	128
Threading The Dawn	129
Rocking Africa	130
The Joy of the Cherry Brook Childhood	132
Freeze Frames	135
Catching Luckystars	136
Stilled the Water	138
Resurrection Spring	139
Von Doos Gazooks Ape	140
Lapis	142
Triathlon Race	143
My Dad, Sgt Brian G. Hodgkinson	144

Tsultrim Dawa

the tea stall on the border of India
waiting for a brilliant idea
ten cups of chai later, reading a map
almost nodded out for a nap

wanted to visit Bhutan
as a world traveler and the fan
twelve years planned the visit
but on the border without a permit

from Mumbai to New Jalpaiguri
the Gitanjali Express didn't hurry
crossed India from west to east
the train ride was a visual feast

arrived at the north-east gateway
connecting four countries within a day
just sat in a tea room now stalled
sweaty with the squirts and appalled

had been there all alone
a man with a bald head like a dome
sat for some chai and rice
a friendly look on his face

ask if he spoke English
but he could only speak a bit

yet understood my plan
offered to take me to Bhutan

being a Buddhist lama there
he even paid my bus fare
to enter by the city Phuentsholing
the city of Bhutan's queen and king

passed through the Bhutan Gate
festooned with dragons paintings
high up on a Himalayan foothill
the monastery like a jewel revealed

he took us up in a Suzuki van
the elevated view was like heaven
visited his Karbandi Monastery
the beginning of a new story

Buddhist lama & Christian priest
are likewise the earth's tourist
tuned together by the universal sign
no wise person could malign

The Four Flags Of Easter

going to the store
drove the blue van out of the basement
car garage
look to the left on the side bank going up
around the stack of cement blocks
four daffodils like cheerful suns
standing tall on new green stems
from the vaporized leftovers of winter
announcing the resurrection of spring
winter like a windy guest
refusing to go with the baggage of
death of frost snow and ice
but the daffies beamed easter is here
shining their light into the heartland
flowering my sunny green siesta

That's All Folks

I blew the wad

the sloshy gray-matter whispers
specks out of eight knobby fountain-pen fingers
cluck the thumb spacer
for days to morning doves coo and chew
the seeds berries of snail siestas

titles slimed up from the suck:
the shaggy dog
the rolling hamster
the vexacious cat's caterwaul

orbs spun the headstand
into the sockets
voices choke in the chest cavity
graffiti spray the bone-dome
the weeping willow masked back to
the giggle of the soloist
echoing the hairs on the arms
to rise, pirouette
and salute

now a sound clangs the cage's ribs
that's all
folks

Freckle Face

from bugs bunny saying what's up doc
siesta down rabbit holes to carrot a tan
break from the head the musty lock
like a dog off the rope and out for fun

surprised by the hair you dyed from the rust
with purple and frizz green blends curled young
the freckles reminding the orange-red of the head
to sing of your magnetic face like the sun

from sighing at you with the utmost eye
dressed in the skirt pleated cream-white
you invited me in to voyeur spy
gaga with your charis style

with kabuki moves so fluid - mystique in the smile
the fingers, hands, wrists, and arms arching flex
beguiling with hips, the legs, waist, and sway
eavesdropping on you better than specs

Hail To the Source

hail to the source
the inner room sanctum

clap to the stream
descending in the core

the higher beckons
to the lower like

the ocean to
the river fanning streams

from whence come
the imaginings and dreams

their waters of refreshment
hail back to the source

like the sea of dust
in dark black of space

the pin pointed stars
broadcast their place

as the rising of the wind
from treelined clouds

for the puff inside
receives the zephyrs

but only if the doors
and the windows ajar

breathing deep the Marconi
watered electric air

mucous less by the siesta
unclogging fare

for the here-body
and all the indoor eye light

big head not asleep
by the vacant cranial night

alive to the core's sight
of the over source

piercing the viscera
like a light-saber sword

Disestablishmentarianism

The establishment is at it again
machinery clanking along like a wobbly tractor-tank
combine sickle blades chewing with old chipped teeth
the religious-philosophical meddling in affairs of the state
not of religion only for the zealots of philosophies
froth at the mouth too, remember

it wasn't religion that killed over one hundred million
people, murdering them in the
name of their philosophies in the twentieth century
but there is no cure for stupid if history is ignored

sewing a 1600s 1700s or 1800s moth-eaten cloth
to patch a new Vera Wang designer dress
the fabrics will shrink and expand differently
ripping away from each other

is the erudite utopian philosophy having the outcome
intended by the manifesto authors - just a question
the establishment, the institution, the crystallization, the fossil
heads cast in concrete - cone shaped
back-handed-hairy-knuckle-mud-dragg   ing

yes, the establishment is at it again
the youth of the 1960s and 70s had it pegged
the cold-war establishment, military industrial complex

squares lock-stepping nose-led by phony money-grubbers
wearing three-piece suits or school and church robes

thumping their dusty leather books, constitutions
or philosophic card-carrying flesh-stamping traditions
in the high ceiling hierarchical citadels of power
pontiff-like beast-like monarchistic oligarchical
bigbrotheristic

Game of Bones

the bipedal bighead glom-stare at royalty
as if the creme de la creme solves our misery
the most ugly annals in world history
are the telling of rank assumes the divine mandate
silver spoon in the mouth spoiled-brat royalty
kings and queens squished all counted under their fate
lived in the lap of siesta sumptuousness
on the ivory tables spread
with the heads of their so-called favoring rest
peons for beheading at their blue-blood behest
tip of the spear philosophic leaders foment world wars
as per Darwin awaiting the jump to the next stage
Kellogg and Nietzsche spur racial eugenic rage
king and queens, chairman, presidents, and ministers
now turning the twenty-first century page
but the twentieth century,
the most bloodshed in history
humankind unkind to the planet, animals, and their own
with shrunken head gray matter leaving all to the throne

Laugh

a blossom has entered my sphere
a flower has bloomed in my world
pollen has sprinkled my ear
yellow
the honey pours out from my eyes

marigold you are
brown earth you are
you are lapis lazuli eye of the sky
and white cotton
above them -
the child inside, blonde haired, you are
and all this the belly laugh of the world.

A Kiss to the Sky

'warms the cockles of my heart' I laugh
at that old line
but just now
on my 2x4 wood porch, seated on my metal
spring bouncing chair
leaned my head back and looked up
the treetops
arrange into an upper slot
like an eye
green leaves, the rim
of my observatory
clouds the whites
blue blue blue
the center orb of the sky
I cannot begin to font-paint how deep
how true an otherworldly hue
cornflower azure turquoise ocean
laughing back into my brown dots
like the love love love
of my in love siesta life
head straight back
looking up
blow
a cockle-warmed heart-shaped
kiss to the sky

Lamplighter

I salute the most high with a bow
the green branch to the vine
on a knee, knees, or face to the ground
or dance with hands in the air
talking as friend to a friend
like a child to a father
you see me
living spring
the lamplighter, the all-seeing eye
chest and head, the temple courts
you pour yourself into the upturned palms
like mother feeds the beaked nestling
heart
folded under siesta wings
content

Mary Yoders

gratefulness
the Amish buffet spread
of broasted chicken and popcorn shrimp

recipes
the Pennsylvania Dutch
of Mary Yoders kitchen feast full

you and me
eyes bigger than bellies
the homemade bread steams to the table

honey squeeze
peanut butter, apple
culinary aphrodisiac

glowing eyes
lock together, feeding
us our succulent siesta plate

set table
springboards coffee splash
for the third May rice confetti lake

Woodwoses

follow me on the forest bed leaves
scraping claw-like nails on the bark of trees
sit down between the snaking roots of the stump
fastening the networked ground
with ropes and threads
pad barefoot on the river weeds like me
as camouflaged woodwoses unclothed unseen
hiding on the ragged edge of the world scene
see with me the submarine frog balloons
the throaty croak
view & be air-dropped off the beaten path
called against the grain, quit the grid till
down in the frond siesta
tired and covered with mud

Reflection

to mossy rooftop to tree filled yard
all confetti with leaves and seeds
around the grass the timber fence
next door the golfers ride their carts

beyond this tangle-wood walnut trail
toward the lake wood snow-belt town

survey the warming earth in bloom
the maple tree helicopter seeds whirl
the apple trees flowering in may
with fluffy pink petals up and down the street

the look out my second-floor window glass
as I from my cold shower pass
in this overgrown forest cottage home
reflecting how long

Enter My Cantillating Den

here I sit
in my den like a bear
with less hair, just downed Yoder's
elixir mixed with seltzer I burp
up letters from four eyes in a processing frame

this den with harmony guitar from goodwill
bought for thirty bucks dates back
the 1960s, I strum strum made up songs
o yea, the statue of an eagle bust eyeballs me too
side a black spinnable globe
inlaid with mother-of-pearl continents, Australia now

glitters the eye, above my screen, the painting
of my wartime pow dad painted by a fellow pow
named nethercote in 1943, dad's been gone since
1999 but still here in the painting his eyes off to the
rightside

I like typing on the old smith corona electric
typing my calendar with this humming machine
skill to change the ink ribbon eraser cartridge

staring at the left wall (like dad, think about that !!)
a jig cut Russian vinyl music record in the stenciled
out shape of snoopy flying his sopwith camel, this
comes from Ukraine over the words
the best way to predict the future
is to create it

It Really Bites

With no idea the 'ell I set in motion,
I stole the coin and fold-up cash out
of dad's grimy work pants
to buy my new coolness.

He'd shower in the basement after work,
I'd sneak down
snake my grubby little hand
into the big front right pocket and try not
to jingle the coins. I fished
around for the paper wad

The single notes, fives, tens, the twenties
and a fifty or even a hundred
next to a few ratty
peppermint lifesavers
and a greasy whittled down
roofing pencil.

I snatched some of the big stuff
now and then, but
pillaged dad's
quarters, the smaller stuff, with
tens and twenties
only now and then.
me, being pretty smart

After six months of my pickpocket rampage,

I amassed the looted brass
of seventy-five dollars
ample boodle
to talk turkey with the cool kid at school,
Ricky, selling

A Lil Indian.
I bought the cool-looking mini bike.
feeling proud of myself
for all my patience
and diligent thievery
I'd worked too hard to steal all that scratch

The bike worked perfectly for Ricky
when he showed it off to me
rubbing my hands
I forked over the moolah

But not when I got it home - nada
yanked the start rope until blisters.
The two-and-a-half horsepower
Briggs and Stratton lawn mower engine
wouldn't turn over.

Ricky cheated me. Livid,
I prayed that the cheap-skate scoundrel
be bitten hard on the buttocks by Karma

It worked...

I've got the teeth marks to prove it.

Riding the Canadian at Twelve

From Ontario, heads west,
those Canadian rails--
sit on my thin cot berth,
stare out the dome car glass
passengers snore at rest
by silvan grass, by lakes
hum flowing with the trees
the opal mountain mists
a smorgasbord of sight
then a sand desert waste
blazing Moose Jaw Bone Creek
the endless stretch of plains
watering station stop
the rocking screech of steel
lulling me doze and wake
outside turquoise for sale
slide-shows flash thru glass
spinning kaleidoscope
careen the mountain pass
Jasper pine wood forest
the dark blue pristine sky
black bear fish a stream
under dewy cedars
eyes chalked full, what I've seen
those carriage wheels turned.

Turkey Bones

songs of gratia rise as sweet incense
from a few hearts of the children of men
& this siesta temple head of mine
to the father's sun citadel of sky
for mother earth's green lands and fields
harvesting the full-hand measure to store
flooding the market storehouses
yet winced and groaned by the
dark floods of war,
broken by metal blows of bloody fists,
eyeless bombs, and thirsty swords
grazie - you still stand stalwart, unbowed,
but fevered by the human fevered pitch
military-industrial polluting of land and sea;
winced and choked by the mountainous bins
of toxic radioactive waste and refuse,
let me shed the bony head & rock-filled chest
before the gifted days of the gracious light are up
& the last fire purges

Hand Puppets

I've doodled outside of the lines
flouting the common accepted designs
defied every postal cardboard box
to the bullying talking heads, the pox
my liberty to make all the choices
power to ignore the discordant voices
nose-to-tail wildebeest race over a cliff
their bones in a valley from a butt sniff
but I march to a different drummer
I won't wince by some foxy max mummer
while there's time, I dance my own rhyme
even if some bird-brains call it a crime
life is too short to squander on them
I won't let the riffraff cut the nerve stem

Siri Means Concealed in Swahili

writing the digital network pen,
the megaphone roars from mouse-like cries,
the news outlets smear the other ten,
wily, spinning up more juicy lies.

machine head kids loitering the street
handhelds infest breakfast brains early,
hive linked by backdoor eye pads for lunch,
the apple worms the sockets hourly

revolutionary, the phonies
want to trashcan the human stories
divided like the Whigs and Tories
closed off to any objective queries

like Chaz and Chop nonaligned zones
dusty old dream effigy burned bones
goosestepping to pushed Marxist theories
aired as the pc tv series

Good Spell

My words are all a jumble, but few fitting verbs I choose
the inward light assemble I fragmentary use,
crumbs off the table of an old rock n roll muse

Atlas holds up the heating world, turning sore
earth's inhabitants now weighing more
an overcrowded planet must to the sky implore

seven thousand years almost to the day
the spinning orb the same it surely cannot stay,
in a high becquerel valley, all the bones will lay.

but not all our roots belong to one bloodline vine,
those by whose confession take the bread and wine,
tied by the life-giving invisible red twine.

Fruit of the womb from the desert virgin maid,
whose prophesied birth made all kings afraid.
Who by the sword cut infants as they played

by the blades of soldiers; hear the horse's snorts,
bloodthirsty butchers kill in field sports;
calculate the slaughter from a birthday's sorts.

but failed at this, the serpent's infernal task,
the pretender hiding behind an evil smiling mask;
blushed from hellfire in which they dance & bask.

Adam, the first progenitor representing us,
riding the zodiac with wheeling Pegasus,
drinking snaky Kool-Aid since the genesis.

but now a new species not of this gene-pool lake,
the second Adam crushed - an asbestos robe to make
the beauty of the Lamb's merit, all are free to take

this news the great commission; now, the logos-word I bring
by this my tongue set on fire: now my heart takes wing,
And now the goodspell to discerning ears I sing.

The Bridge Once Lifted

like the very air I breathe
the book's song sings the light
it's the voice standing in back of me
& the center point of this dark world

the pierced hand holds mine
at this sacred footstool of the divine
blood for blood on a carpenter's tree
rusty spikes tacking a crossbeam
riving bones tendons and sinew
hung on the butcher's meat hook

raked with a whip with razor shards
streams of red filming the eyes
needle thorns pin the skull

this, the altar table where
the propitiations's parts laid out
between the firmament's horizon
& this weedy damaged earth
he is now the bridge once lifted

Core Gardening

the mouth speaks from the calling heart
artless at first, the sprouting rose,
core gardening is an art
the seedbed to disclose.

hate or love inflames the tongue,
plucked daisy petals seldom lie
from their sown germination sung,
waved in the bluing sky.

if from a pestiferous soil essayed,
its deep-seated purpose reach—
the germ's voice the tongue obeyed,
to blossom poisonous speech.

make the distinction, child of earth
each source performs its part,
cultivation is a garden's worth
from the center of the heart.

Morte-Saison Gone

awaking from the ice-crusted morte-saison
(the tranquilized hibernation not so dear!)
the greening spring rejuvenating everyone
down to the cellar goes the holiday beer
after the christened mead & late year guerdon
of apple glazed ham and stuffed turkey cheer
(another stardate click in the perennial orbit gone!)
whining not as good as yesteryear.

what now changed for the earth snow lay upon?
(what now needs the lawn's mowing gear?)
the sun's heat undressing & redressing everyone
dogs and cats shed, gym rats with overweight fear
the ruddy skin not screened to the poison sun
cabin fever replaced by Easter spring fever cheer
(short-shorts showing buttock in fashion)
the same mating dance of yesteryear.

what have these workaday years won?
with Saturn, Venus & the moon near!
after the earth thaws, ice once lay upon,
the feat of sunning earthworms under the clear
after the tree-toppling winds & rain's valor done?

that transformation is not a mere
chance, but the seasonal incubation paragon
never like the dried-up ghosts of yesteryear.

the new creation renovation is done
spring spurring all to good cheer
for what is already morte-saison gone
is yesteryear.

Mom Dear

The lady putters
her morning lakefront yard
on
her daily rounds to feed the backyard feral cats
that sleep in the makeshift shed.
Like the pied piper
she calls them in Latvian
to the front door for milk.
Also saves leftover scraps
on crumpled foil tins
for the evening birdseed-thieving raccoons
and the munchie possum.
Noisy birds flock the trees by her locked sliding
glass window;
iridescent hummers and bully bluejays,
headbanging woodpeckers, sunny finches,
and Ohio cardinals.
With her green thumb, she clips bits of leaves just outside
the screen door
stoop,
sage, cilantro, rosemary and basil
for the food
in her kitchen pots that fragrance the house
for the afternoon visitors.
The little old house
that once housed six

but now
only the indoor
giant cat
and the ninety-year-old young,
her.

Workaday Commute

Talk to the clock on the cellphone
Chase the rat race like a juicy bone
Coffee the brain to the highway thrum
People talking at you like a drum.

Traffic helicopters circle overhead
Gawks slow for car holding the dead
To punch in at seven, cars push and shove
Morning work mashup boxing gloves.

Pass rundown downtown, east-side to west
Drive by slum dog houses for the roach infest
Flip the radio to an oldie song
The morning haze smog covers the throng.

The rat race red-face triggers everyone
Counting the days the same under the sun
Just another day in paradise of shoddy food
After evening work, I'll siesta the wood.

But stead, after trading hours for dollars
I press my shirts of blue and white collars.

Fire Wood

Echoes
Reverb after the axe struck the trunk,
And the thudding!
Cleaved to the center like jackhammers.

Syrupy sticky
Sap coated the little wedge-chip caves, like
Blood oozed,
Remembered the root-thread capillary grammar
Under the pulp

That waved and rustled green
Rungs of years;
Abandoned to stump, eaten by bracket fungi;
Passed, I sit on the roadside stool.

Like neutering verbs tongue-shot
From pursed lips
Chop firewood, forest-dragged
Wiener roast bonfire.

A Fiesta

I'm a plain man
ever on siesta
laid back and chill.
The remembered lights
Like unanswered holograph mail
Still call;
Still knock;
silver-
screened on the wall from my bone-visor
eyes
like sentient mists and shades
of the living
deceased.
I see their markers
burial plots
but
they still speak;
order me to sit
up
fly straight,
I argue with them
too.
the voices echo
from
glossy faces
with dogeared corners

of 35mm paper,
yellowed
from age
slipped in brittle plastic
sleeves.
as
I
began,
I'm a plain man
ever on fiesta
Dia de los Muertos
carrying on
dialogues
with my past.

Heavy With Children

the dwarf apple tree seems very different now
it holds loads of heavy children aloft

and though its tired limbs hang
down lower from the strain
the expression of plume glows from the scarred gnarled trunk
as ornaments incubate in a late summer sun

the other trees are harps strummed by zephyr
conducting orchestras of leaf-eating insects

a woodpecker being the percussionist
the audience of black-eyed susans with gold
around their singular drooping eyes

while small white butterflies catch rides
the upcoming-storm currents of afternoon wind
the flutters searching for flowering mates

the yellow-jacket apple tree watches and waits
leaning the siesta
to the right

The Lot

the dog and I
under the old blue-eye
our circuitous boon
on many a lazy afternoon

behind the boarded businesses
along the roots of stunted trees
and the broken flight
of the failing bees

the bumbles don't waggle-dance
having the fuzzy appearance
nosed by the yelping suspense
too near the lions of the fence

border to the petroleum banks
of the rainbow scum pond
once waded by the watchman
the great blue heron

crunched Pepsi cans
overflowing dumpster bins
soggy sofas left to rot
the dog and I walked the parking lot

Flatula-Dracula

first date after sixty two days
we bought tickets for
this autumn near the falls
the ninety-third year
of the little theater
does Bram Stoker's Dracula
seven thirty the curtains lift

we stop for dinner of spinach
and medium pink steak
Gorgonzola blue cheese on salad
a second floor window overlooking the town
with the gazebo and 1800s craggy buildings
the setting sun dotting the clouds

bon appetite we walk down Franklin street
past the funeral home, this night of the Tiger's
home coming, then to the stuffy theater
to pasty-face the flat gassy Dracula

not soon enough
we off like a cat on a hot tin roof at
intermission to depressurize
so unceremoniously

Lucky Stones

the yellowed photographs still stereoscopic to me
behind the eye
washed into the film
of my brain like
the arrowheads found by my uncle displayed in glass
windowed wood boxes
he found in Ohio valleys, gorges, and near lakes
the day by a brook
he found a megalodon tooth
as his chief prize
I, too, with sharp eyes
fossil hunted and looked
for arrowheads and a trilobite mold
but only found milky and rosy quartz
lucky stones
and fool's gold

Morning Salute

this morning

you
the vine

of the trees the maples the oaks the sweetgum
the Chinese aspen basswood buckeye and chestnut

of the clattering cicada serenading the sun

of the siesta porch stoop with metal spring chair

of the chirping chatty robin the hasta el fuego hummingbird
overhead screaming eagle and mourning dove covid coo

the black gray and brown squirrels walking
the rough timber fence

of the marigold exploding from out of the boxes
and the chipmunks burrowing making a mess

you da vine, large and in charge, the dime bag high
of me falling for a towhead girl with bright eyes

the flitter flutter fuzzy flux inside the solar plexus and
of the head that doesn't know what's nexus

da vine of da Vinci this morning
I salute you

The Displacements of War

a family of six are hunkering down in a dank cellar
the mother and father were issued Kalashnikovs
enough for the older children to use
if necessary,

rats have already begun
sharing the food they've stored
they wait for more sounds of shelling
and distant explosions that seem to be getting nearer

the father and mother love their land
but part of them questions sickeningly
if they should've

evacuated with the others because they face
an oncoming monster with only one

outcome

Note to Self

Brian is wearing
a t-shirt colorfully written
"Red barns, White fences, Blue jeans"
signed Bob Evans— bought after
a three cheese omelet with eight
sticks of bacon.
On a greening spring day,
not knowing why.
He's also wearing beige jeans
with cornflower blue socks—fashionista
he's not. Looking at his whiskered mug
in the mirror, sees some new
forehead lines like a park trail map,
and scowls, too, at his crumpled frizz mop.
Brian's note to himself " Well, this is that—yes,
this is that."

Bottomless Cup

Cafe from maître d'hôtel
scents the house french roast
the ceramic mug topped off black
the tonic toasts the cottage cheese cockles
warm, November snow blankets the yard
just a week after Indian heat of seventy five.
Bed-seated
gulping down java brew the bitter dark
the impending holiday lights mirror back
shout from the clattering kitchen
alongside the meow of the tortoiseshell
kitten, do you want more coffee
4 the bottomless cup?

Morning Stroll With the Cat

up the foyer stairs with the tan-streaked cat
the golden girl stands in the boudoir mirror
rubbing down with skin oil from Trader Joe's shop
then putting the kitten in the black zipper mesh stroller
for a jaunty jaunt outside in the sun's autumn glow
for the indoor stink, off with a brisk windy blow
back in the house, the granite top kitchen
savory breakfast: sausage and maple syrup
mom's zucchini muffin, coffee, & chai tea
the soft meowing for a cat treat toll

Feast Before Famine

chirrups and twitters
the plastic Christmas gift bird house
full of sunflower seeds, pine nuts
chomped by a fat gray squirrel
chewing in the New Year
hunger

Alghaba

walking the yellowed woods of this neon world
no ventilation for the smoking den smog sky
grass the locust and ticked sycamore trees
brackish waters with fossil fuel slick
rainbow from oily black skyscraper tile pipes,
hives of gunmetal cement sport a schoolhouse,
school of paralysis passing the mantel of loss;
lost graffiti slipped on the banana peel streets
mellow-yellow, cocaine envelope hand-off,
buggy pin pricked, a crossfire cap,
new blooms plucked at the root.

haiku #2

people talk   flap gums
pointing earth's money castles
tawdry by   dozens

Rainbow Dorothy

woman with rainbow hair
joking called her his unicorn girl
powder blue to gray
eyes depending on the light her nose
regal and large
in her catacomb steeple house home
she's busy refinishing antiques like armoires
with a little Toto-like dog with a cute yellow bow
awestruck to finally siesta meet in the flesh
the woman with the rainbow hair
an old sailor envisioned in his cups but the
unicorn out of his league

Red Lined

The line of demarcation
divides
two grounds of soil,
two places to stand; first,
the deck of a sinking ship
flying black then red colors
anchored at pirate bay
on the left death side
of the yard arm,

Or the potting soil
on the green side - starboard
of the stanchion yard arm;
the ground of expiation and
pest removal, gangway to the deck of
the asbestos-pitched ark - fitted
with fire-proof rigging.

The dividing line is a red thread over
thousands of years kept
trailing through the mass cemetery

to the ground of the empty tomb.

An Unwanted Visitor

With dark black mask, ringed fur of gray,
Raccoon shadows float to and fro
Here within the corn crib room
The coon looks spectral with whisker plume.
Inside the grain shed, hand over hand, slow —
The chaff drops, the dusty spray.
His climbing night bump is magnified,
For the quietude of night holds his rein;
Footfall from the farmer the silence breaks,
The munching coon with new stealth awakes,
And from the upper rafter shimmies down again,
To spy his clear route to take off outside.
He looks out a chink across the barnyard lawn,
To the hunkered down chickens in their coop;
The crib is trashed, undone by his hands,
Full of dung, chewed husks and stalk strands

Topper

I am a space-time traveler
on my way to who-knows-where
like a roller-coaster at the county fair
flying off the calendar
several billion clicks I've clocked so far
sucking earth's satellite air
orbiting this sun flare star
like a dreidel top spinning who-knows-where

Zum-Zum

zum-zum
frankincense and myrrh
clic with the in-breath
out, follow like Buddha's flower
luve the purr sound, do ya now
the body filling siesta senses
all ow leg go, leg g-d
lettuce bray not spray
frank einstein with jar encased brain
take all with a grain,
or swivel down the drain
this poetic purple rain
dah cerebellum crazy train
the mad cow murrain
horse hay woodbine
why not try to spiel bind
the aerie skies time-blind (?)

aftermath

castles minced to bone
the slap crack
blood crush of loss
eyes mirror ash

the phoenix stares down
from blood roots of powdered heart
saw me swearing

It Started With One Bag

walnuts in the shell
the whole bag tossed on the lawn
gray and black squirrels

scratching sound porch door
the squirrel teeth to chew more
pantry is empty

squirrels lined a row
on the patio long bench
the fans of the house

old peanut butter
tails shaking the eyes bugging
squirrel siesta

hundreds of squirrels
with plans to pirate the house
squirrel brigands rise

Strutting Her Hightops

after hours, went in the circle-k for a beer a forty eight magnum
the cashier a flower arrangement ogled the cut of her shape
gyroscope the eyes out of sync overtook into puppy staring
schoolboy she smiled at me her purple hair
the high-top canvas tennis shoes
asked me to early morning dinner after work that stirred
the embers creator created the indomitable appetite

that undressed a siesta on the tower
of paris

the theaters of losangeles

and the marine drive with bollywood starlet in bombay

but this sweetheart - full of life - with her undulating machine oiled
& smooth strutting her poetry - lit the lamp post
of my..

..now that beer

Woodlore Easter Eggs

the goodwill thumb worn bookshelf of adverbs
flooding over, but not the forest for a tree
as the rabbit zigzags by with a cheekful of grass
the hunters loaded for bear laugh down at them
too peter-like for their man cave trophy rooms
but they cannot see
if the chapped hikers are hitched
and not ankle deep in bruin scat just dumped
the wordsmith hunter on unpaid siesta
able to orient self
turns the nose from constipated tracker
snobs (for larger heads their manuals make)
--leaves for toilet paper or the goodwill
for woodlore doesn't fud the beech and the beach

but blanc the bunny rabbit
for the lights of pricked up ears
pinpoints you

with easter eggs

Underwater Pictures

I reach to the quick, he said. I reach it with my camper;
Do not sink afraid.
I do not run: I sit here.

That if the sea burst in upon me?
Do I chum the titanic abyss?
Like a bubble pops I kiss the floor.

The five are a shadow.
How the aquatic fed on the surface fauna
Every squid for a quarter mil. How?

Listen: the gong the sonar piqued: sub merge
Clunk like a metal balloon fut.
The gate to the wreck fattened the giant.

The quick and then ocean dead;
Shades join the iceberg-sunk crew
Ship bones as a pillow.

I siesta by my radio. The report after days
Chills my bones; calls into my head
Underwater pictures.

A Tub of Reciprocity

The sprocket recipe, charis plus eros
Pinch of philia udders Greek agape.
Trade, the siesta doorway
To ever-after sunbathed
Horizon of the duo that are here
Now, brown cow

Pass the soap and take the scrub a nub
You part me, I wax you in the tub
From even the wind, the lungs
Air of joined spheres.

Vibratory drums, all the thrums
Wrestling against the longest thumbs
If and when, the bosom-muscle numbs,
Leopard feathered paddles, speak
in tongues

eclipse

the stars are eclipsed by the noxious fumes rising
from the rubble of a missile-gutted
civilian apartment building
containing the mangled body of a five-year-old
still holding her doll in a death clutch
while five thousand miles away,
another five-year-old girl in kindergarten
opens her lunch box to find
her mom's note
with a smiley face I love you

The Reaper

the wanton slaughter begins
hacking, hewing, and spewing
millions are just vaporized
a green mist covers the scene
grim returns them to the dust
to fertilize the earth's soil
under their children that rise
a new fertile crescent to grow
like weeds with wild flowers
clover bluebells and daisies
rapeseed listrum and knapweed
their raison d'être calling
the mower to pass

The Poet Gripped by a Raven

judicious hunter of the sky,
corvid of Gehenna's lie,
helping wolves for rancid scraps.
fights with rats the bulk of cats;
jet-black wraith pick-pecks a bone,
mynah-like, its voice intones.
flicks a tilt -- A questioning look?
'Nevermore,' rejoined the crook.

Alfred's Sound Bite; Take One

The worldwide web bangs at the door:
Screened in eyes and ears and head,
I press the button when I stretch at four;
Lulls me to sleep when I go to bed.

The hivemind kids on the street
Glued to glittering handheld devices
Like a gaggle of sheep, goad ears to a bleat
Nerve centers for every crisis.

Viral tubes and flaming twits
Shrinking the heads of the hap-less,
Suckling nobs, posing bits
Saps, like dead branches, sapless.

From the buttock, rung and buzzed
Like a cow prod, over and again,
Drapes skull with a type of braining fuzz
If it not squeezing now, binging when.

Once upon then, the newsprint of the press
The machine for opine-pickling the breast.
But now a gadget of candy bar size
Tinkers the bone-dome wetware nest.

The Sun Swings Itself

the light bulb flickers on

with requester of the sunlight
for the morning head

the commenter jumbles
a syllable or two to label

the barking dog next door
that invaded the sleep sightings

the whining bladder and smoldering
stomach juices

the face of the cat ogling birds
on the hump of the upstairs window

couch

the lung-biting remnants of a covid cough
morning attack

and the swirling electric
questionmark

in the beetle-brow forehead.

plan for the day?

Traffic

home staring at a screen
fishing for poetic inspiration
half listening to airheaded
shock-jock talk radio
eating a makeshift supper of antipasto
from a grocer-labeled plastic container
siesta-hunting for literary building blocks
like sweet cherry bonbons

the gray elevator not quite reaching the top
fingertips type staccato, but tripe and trash
stink out,
the cheese and stale salami butt ends
hide pieces of grizzle,
face me,
the man in the mirror
standing, stagger to the window

brushing the lampshades,
open the livingroom louver blinds
trying to cook up a verse or two
but see nothing

climb into the automobile at dusk,
cruise the inner city avenues
see inked girls sashay in short dresses
the naked pavements,

the traffic

The Marina Cat

the marina cat
lived on the fisherman's wharf
snarfing garbage of rotting fish heads
the green chitlins of skinned walleyes
black and orange tortoise shell coat
joker smeared tan lip
mask-like nose, nostril tips
underweight for a year old adolescent
five pounds wet just skin and bones
abused with a cracked front tooth
in mottled fur
now growing into her longish tail
too small for it
the marina cat

The Gut Punch

the gut punch
hollow tickling ache
the chest cavity boxing
the solar plexus
fluttery and breathless

suitcases all packed and stretch out
just for a wee siesta
luxury cruise comps dancing
across the eyelids
the sleepy eyes do not see the wrist
head woozy not screwed on

what! the eyes bug out on stems
thump down the stairs like a madman
while dressing - flag a taxi
shout, gun it!
more money for the driver

run like a gazelle from the taxi to the dock
but the transatlantic liner just embarked
cresting the wave without a passenger
standing alone on the empty pier
staring at the ticket

if only if only echoing eyes wet

driving back home kicking self as a heel
a world-sized fail crushing the back

sitting in the living room bored
disappointment eaten
tuned in the tubed radio

the flash report on every station

titanic sank

Stained

mid-afternoon
wander
following the floating
dandelion seed parachute
rides an alternative breeze,
in
stained-glass knock-off nike

off to the left,
waxy purple, red, yellow, & pink tulips
caressing the nose floral perfumes
fuzz-buzzers buzz
&
the odor of heating moist black soil
is airing a wormy report for
teem mulch

mineral fortify
the sun-bathing
upturned face
dandelion

& those stained

The Watchman On the Shadowy Decks

The watchman on the shadowy decks
of memory
just the face is the treasure
like moonlight bejewels the ocean's surface

suction-cupped tentacles yank down down down—
leviathan breakers wash over
crest into throat and lungs.
scan the horizon for the lighthouse.

rising, a beam of light
plunging, the black ink

deep swallows to deep
nightfall
the sea's engraved lockets
the picture of the yellow flower in the hair
with the anchor's chain of the Dutchman
the necklace

Vengeance is Mine

the dust settles after a missile blast
sleeping sons and daughters to black ashes passed

shredding the youths flowering petal
the faces of death from grey gunmetal

scribbled play notes of a worn down pencil
silenced throats of the cut paper doll stencil

Sponge Bob seen on a living room screen
the late air raid siren ululates a scream

A Father's Prayer

A father's prayer:

Jesus, Beloved, Jesus, Beloved, Jesus, Beloved...
Jesus, Light, Jesus, Light, Jesus, Light...
Jesus, Princess, Jesus, Princess, Jesus, Princess...
Jesus, Treasure, Jesus, Treasure, Jesus, Treasure...

like an unnamed request
whispering
the pictured names with the breath -
tying into the breast's core beat...
then interwoven strands braid a shield.

plus-sign

sun-prisms a kaleidoscope on the reading room walls
from the cut glass cross shape of a plus sign
this crystal thrones the window sill
the splaying out of gain and loss
yes the fuss budgets fuss their fuss
by their head trips lost
but I
only trust

Digest

I go to the restaurant
buy the bacon and eggs
this is it

the green light turns yellow
stop the van at the red
sit the long red light
my eyelids flutter shut
I see
she walks in the forest with me during the fall
this is it

eyeballs pop open
how long were they shut
the red light still red
this is it

the darkening road
as the nightfall dims the trees
this is it

the evergreens look black
other trees
naked and gray even in april
this is it

steering the dodge caravan down pettibone road
pass the mother hen farm sign saying fresh eggs for sale

maple syrup
this is it

the pines look dark and sinister
no back road streetlights
passing a house with the sign
blind-squirrel farm
next to a lake
this is it

home on the sofa noshing on the three-egg
omelet
chewing down strips of bacon
this is it

the stomach is full the eyes go behind lids
siesta satis faction
this is…

No Laughing Matter

After school clubs with jack flash
red-faced smiling bearded satanimp
role-modelling…
This club after the rainbow afternoon drag
reading of Gay B C's
and privy counseling about if
gonadal removal fits my six-year-old
uncooked callow brain
but don't tell the parents after-all
the grooming schools toys-4-us
now re-education camps to brain wash
out the junk mom and dad hold on to.

Fox made matching grants for this.

A Coup Fourré

I'm bone-tired of liars
that bellow
their socalled soshe wokeness
while
shadow-banning
anyone
they argue with
thoughtpolicing by net fiat
covering the mass un-
mindednesses with
poison scare-tactic webs
baiting
lying
baiting
crucifying
lese-majesty
while the true die in the streets.

A Beachcomber

I walk a beachcomber trackless path
footsteps erased by the sea
no path back to the craggy past
years measured by a tree
leathery skin, raisin-like in the sun,
now and then, a manta ray ride,
yesterday a bluffing windfall won
buried in the sand to hide,
not planning out a day
the seashells shining plain,
washed up with the next swell
over and over again,
toes sink the cold sand at night–
the ocean moon water-song light.

Out Like a Lamb

The sweetbay and star magnolia
trees in the front yard by the
paved drive,
pushed out white
and purple-pink blooms this spring
suffusing scents both night and day.
But as this hazy wildfire-smoked
Spring outs like a sooty lamb,
the water lily blossoms fertilize
the loam
while from my lungs
coughing up foam.

The Call of Nature

I've a coxcomb red rooster pate
That cockcrows with spurred rooster legs
And morning struts atop the barnyard fence
With my flushed reddish orange clawed pegs

I assist the hens to lay eggs
And chase those clucking gals all around
True to the pecking order, she begs
Holding her down with beak to the ground.

[the sun lights day]

the sun lights day
the moon the night
gravitation is just this
every star burns out
with nova light
and nothing is amiss

Lilo

the inflatable jitterbugs atop
swelling mountains of ink
then coasting down
into the valley maws

air bubbles out holes
pin-pricked submerging
trying to ride out the storm

burning lungs lips pursing
cough pressure into the sag
of the rubbery life raft
pumping it up with gasps

the whirlpool rotates
hours and days

Aegis

The earth stabbed,
star dance with the chaosmos
the glut of the light-drawn moth
with its night chill shadow
eyed wings for the onlooker
but mark its chutzpah
to press its panoply
on the unwary,
not presuming
such brazen monarch, the voyeur
siesta tree house
for the greening spring,
from the stinging lash
of its saddle bags

Cat Watching Birds

flitting
flapping
chirruping
hopping
picking
pecking
flitting
chipping
looking
gobbling
swallowing
winging

Beyond Spacetime, We

bloodstreams flow
I and you
breathe that moist burned tobacco breath into me
you the chic smoker eau de toilette
but the blue wisp is just you
lungs share the in-breath, whoosh, back you then me
lips locked, eyes locked, faux masks obliterate
you fart-mouth laugh wet raspberries
but out the nose of mine
bellyaches from the tearful happy howls
but
two heartbeats, the synchronicity
the light and the dark together, irony
playful players, siesta shades of gray
me, like the werewolf
you, the champagne marinated steak
yet, the you-me beaux esprits
metamorphosing electricity
of you, of me &
fire enters
until the sun flares
beyond spacetime, we

Bid a Long Adieu

lying together face to face
on top the mossy knoll
you told me you were going
but you loved me
past adieu

The Grid

the universal grid
enmeshed with the energetic human id
is like the surface of a placid lake
to keep it placid for your own sake
whatever stone you toss into the ring
is sure to return to you again

nothing to give

the sparkle of the sun on the water's surface
the hazy spot in the distance is a ship
fat seagulls ha-ha-ha and scream patrolling the shore
there is a faint fishy scent on the intermittent breezes

scavengers aren't scared of me strolling down the beach
they approach skittishly, eying me for a handout
I carry nothing to give them
yet happily abundant

Amber

I still see their faces
bubbling the gray stuff in my bone head
pictures
like yellowed photographs
the set faces
noses mouths and lips
lines of their bodies

the holographs looking three-d
animated messages
like r2d2 screened the bit from obi-wan
gesticulating thin air

like a museum
of science with
the slab of amber
yellow-orange
translucent
the giant dinosaur mosquito
frozen sculpture

no matter how many years pass
not a day older
that's how I see them

picturing their lives
happy without me

and my today's
the siesta without them

and no black arts
can conjure
that fossil mosquito
to drink blood
again

Crossing Over The Equator

I flew dutch airlines to kakamega kenya
at the age of twenty eight
near lake victoria in east africa
took twenty-two hours to relocate

from the nairobi airport to kakamega
driving five hours by landrover
through the pot-holed roads of kenya
seeing giraffe and herds of zebra

I lived among the luyia tribe
they adopted me as their own
stayed for twenty years, though from ohio
but now share a distant home

I've another loving family
five thousand miles to the east
we see beyond our skins and nationality
we share together our global feast

Have A Look

E nter the burial cave, have a look around

A table of stone, a sunken body shape of wound heavy cloth on it

S un shines in, the stone covering the cave's mouth rolled to the side

T wo sitting bright visages ask - seek for the living among the dead?

E lectric terror, bumping the head leaving quick

R un like the wind to tell the others

Communication

death
war
family feuds
pathologies

from obstructions
of essential pathways

elimination
more critical than
assimilation

toxic collections
clog
crowd out
divide

sun
oxygen
pure water
minerals
xylem root
tissues
conduct water
chlorophyll
in plants

circulating conduits
transporting hemoglobin
the animation of
all animals
sentience

*green & red felicity
*depend
*on
*open
*channels

The Optics

runs amok inside of the head
twittering faces gloating over the dead
thumbing the nose whenever fact-finding tries
to draw the pinocchio-nose on insulting lies

bleeds the balls with the evening news
craps in the kitchen with their monstrous views
winding everyone up the talking-heads
the blaring in the cap when going to bed

floating in lockstep biding the time
slurping up the same old trumpeted slime
repeating-repeating the hogwash is rank
a fleet enema required to purge the bank

Watch Care

After traveling 38 billion elliptical miles, I realize
the watch-care over my life is circumspect.
Like the vibrating atmosphere surrounding the hummingbird,
it swam through yesterday before my lagging eyes.
It had no frown on its metallic blue face while it
poked the Lady Baltimore one by one.

Voyagers

feral roaming
under the dappled
stallion skies
the mustangs of the ocean
stray inland from
the outer ranges to thunder
the jagged shoreline

seagulls ha-ha-ha-ha
atop orange sunset
crested swells
to the
dots of distant ships
carried over the blurred horizon

as once we

Bird Cherry Tree

under the tail squeezed it out
the bird sowed the seed in flight
hit the stone statue splashed white
the rain swept the dot to earth
to the grass between the blades
near the dry sand walking path
into wet soil dug by worms
down yellow-green baby root
drinking the dirty water
rounding back pushing to sun
sticking the bird cherry tree
to stand narrow greening leaves
sprays of flowers and red fruit
the feathered claws eat and poop

Salts

grinned teeth
from ocean floor skulls
whitened
from centuries of restless
seas
pickled by the brine
the vessels of silted
octopus inhabited tombs
of the salt sailors who once set out
to live

Snap

archway with gargoyle
bat wings gremlin face crow feet
grinning knees to ears
the titan's tripwire
squat imp in the ointment jar
the spill of empires
pride goeth before
a crumbling shaking crash
don't lean the laurels
banana fiber
multi strand noose bird feet snare
triggers like lightning

Diamond Girl

gold
anklets
on your
ankles -
silver
bells
on your
toes -
and
I fell
head
over
toes
for you -
how
funny
we
pull-arm
slot
machined
both me
& you
scratched
lotto
tickets
of you & me

slipping
between
the winnings
but
only
to cherry
more lines
of three
ding ding ding
diamond
girl

A Sapphire from Clay

Like the sunlight of that day
on the grasses of light window

out from the institutional shadows
of the yellowed broken blinds

the rustling emeralds of outdoor wood
sings the eyes of sun

for the hearts of fluent men, binary
or not, still are the earth song

these hands squeezed into
a slice of art room molding clay

malleable kneading the folds
for throwing a creature creation

inside a stone hard, but not, a ring
of white gold and blue

the star sapphire like an eye
picked out from the dead grey lump

haiku #6 10-05-2022

shallows of the pond
fording naked to the knees
short toes if the snakes

De Jure

Cherry Brook,
Row boat caught fish to cook
By the angling sand hill crane,
From the wooden dock, I look,
For bluegill cast the wriggling hook,
Stuck in the algae depths again.

Silver shiner spinner reels,
The duck pond mirrors my heels,
Casting bait of jitterbug lure,
Shaped like a metal dragonfly
That near my head strafed by,
Of the cherry tree brook, de jure.

Cat's Eyes

hear the birds
perch trees, swim clouds
flying their circle dance
harp and strings
xylophone voices streamside
flows the current of this moment
Moka the tortoiseshell cat
chirping along with wide staring eyes
elsewhere
in a safe place

Jet Lag Went South

shuck off from the finger tips
shot straight from the hip
pads the bitten print on the home keys
table crumb nuts and screwy pieces
by the jetlag cranial shake it jumble
picks from the night turbulent mumble
falling from the overhead cracks & creases
walking down the airport aisled kiosks
of the coffee drinking corporate empire
flat panel shows the CNN mind vampire
grimacing her grin as she motormouth talks
commercialized customers caper carded cash
sucking green credits from their pinhole gash
mindlessly mulling the mall-like marble halls
neck-pillow tired of sardine can walls
& me, jotting this scribble on the back of a pass
to the silhouette man to flat out held gas
from airline nibbles, what crunched in the mouth
the price I paid, when the jet lag went south

Needles

dismantling the tree
unwinding the garland and lights
silken balls back in the box
the newyear counts
champing upon the day

Slaked

a ladle of liquefied life
dribbles from the pierced hand,
digs a fountain head frothing up;
drink now,
belly-laugh rivers, dervish spins
laved hands in the air,
without the
galling worry weight
unyoked of burden,
schlepping pails of polluted
swamp streams.
the omega now risen. b siesta
water slaked.

Regatta Afternoon

aquamarine sea, the blue sky
whites of giant clouds
marking the lip of the world

webbed foot bird atop the waves
dips bill for a shaky trough
a siesta for a fish

wind-full sails of boats tip heel
slice the foam crests with shark tooth keel
sun-drenched regatta afternoon

the beach sprays misting the face
binoculars to see the race
"Peregrine 1" sloop in first place

Flash Bulb

Through the scrub bush path at night
walk the muddy with my bike
now the sky is strangely bright
a rushing wind, a blinding light

visiting the - tanka

the metal box fan
stomach gas and intestine
run for siesta
feather edged books of poems
hey-google read a haiku

Docking Haiku

When a ship has sailed
the head mooring line falls limp
till a new cruise docks

Green Tongue

green chai tea & sliding glass doors taking in
the smell of summer leaves tobacco in the sun
cornucopia of chlorophyll greens the day
select how to savor, this is it
chew the spicy maple leaf

Sunday Drivers

the van driver spots giveaway furniture
stuff on the roadside tree lawn
near the Auburn Lakes
two porta potty bedpans
toilet pots to piss in
broken chairs cracked
knotty pine shelves
water damaged cloudy mirrors
a senior woman's bric a brac
bygone
discarded treasures

A Nest

scream from atop the maple tree
winging the branches and trunks
eyes like a laser for the high crook
place for the rough egg bed build
an outside basket weave of twigs and leaves
inside cup of soft Spanish moss and grass
the wed couple siesta rest
the bald eagle egg-filled nest

The Sentry

the garden rabbit made of stone
she, a green thumb
that's her rabbit
the sentry over the lavender and chives
the hyacinth and chinese elm
she planted with mint and kale
while she dug and puttered
fertilized and primped
but stone-ears still sitting guard
over the crabgrass and mallow
sandbur and shepherd's purse
quackgrass, black medic & pigweed
for the gardener's been planted 5-years now
she, the larger seed with the bigger sentry

To The Revenant Victor

"to the victor
go the spoils"
when you look back at the Jewish carpenter
from Galilee do you see
a victor?
They say, he healed
by the command
of his voice
and the touch
of his hand.
They say, he claimed
sonship with the most high
that he was convicted as
an inciter and blasphemer
by the Sanhedrin and Pilate
to be crucified as a common criminal.
look back into the past
at this figure tortured and beaten
hung on a wooden cross
nailed through his hands and feet,
do you see a victor?
or see a wrongheaded martyr?
can you agree humankind looks like
it's under a curse? we assassinate
kill maim pillage pollute rape steal
hate bomb knife hijack muck smog

choke betray lie cheat gossip bully
murder destroy - but
a figurehead represented
the whole race
the curse absorber spiked to
the lightning-rod-like tree
don't be tricked -
he won,
revenant

... for you.

Thought Police

figments of the heads
talking as the press off point
with conical skulls

politicians bankers doctors and lawyers
twaddle enunciated lip reading
con artifice cue cards

on the vibrating light screen saber
bushy-brow bobble nog gins
usurping freedom saying they're the pros

the daily rag looping soundbites
braggodocia polar pundits
nonintellectual pretenders

preprogrammed montages
of what's-my-line echochamber babble
of the spin-doctoring

playing the dead bat "I don't recall"
vilifying inquiry conspiratorial
wrestling gnats, swallowing camels

the rhetoric of polit retaliation
demanding one opinion

Still Smiling

The clock hands race the day.
but red lights seem to creep;
trade my time for a pittance pay,
and very little sleep.

Whatever committed was good:
fruits of hard labor mixed.
beside me smiling providence stood,—
I was not perplexed.

Metamorphic

The unmitigated nerve of the cocoons,
fighting the process,
wanton for
the birth not given:
no truce with the constructed false fates,
the sworn enemy of diverse worms
just so skeleton-key bolted closets
and whitewashed tombs may go back
and mirror in-the-eye sanitized
in that before metamorphic
prepubescence for yet
more wasting
of you.

To Javelina & to Hold

a javelina is not a pig
but hog tusk faced in appearance
this one little bed runt, not that big
is my hoof split footed interference

when she lays herself down for siesta at night
the stuffy javelina she hugs so tight
but squeezing myself between her and it
might foment a jealous grunting fit

she holds it and snores, I wait for the nod slip
her snooze snorting sounds like f-f-f aaa haw uk
gentle I jiggle the gray porker out of her grip
holding her skin to mine like a piggy in luck

It May Be Love - Dodoitzu

shared hunger of eyes and cores
two bodies firing as one
joined at the lips, cores, and hips
the earth-walk partners

Tapestries

we are all tapestries hooked and woven
textured rows multicolored and complex
shadings with dangling participles
crocheted comma splices
stitched in double negatives
slipped in verb chaining constructions
defying logical needle-point explanation
with the herring bone
quilted and knitted
when flaws are
as strung beauty
without ignoring that we
cannot untie
since we are all
knotty messes
when viewed from
the raw side

Bust

Glitzy gals bare 4 beads
shallow surface sex is sold
Emma gives in 20 minutes, $39.95 special
shake sensual silicone so seductive
having hungry horny holograms
organs of organic corn corgis
phony-baloney prawn ponies
slips slimy as the slits of slots
fornicating flesh finances fantasies
who hypnotize hollow hordes
giving grotesque gods, goddesses,
idyllic idols of idling idiots
fantastic phantasms phallus
garish gala-glamor grins gross
burlesque bubba-button boys
superficial, artificial, commercial
pulling bling-bling polling poles
diamonds, cherries, and sevens, in a row
flash for finding free-fall cash-flow
seriously suckered sadly insatiable
lustily longing 4
more

Play Today!

just exist?
without expressing?
death...
cold breath
comatose...

dive in the creative river
flowing
another knowing
growing fire
inspiring

now the chance
to dance
your own poem alone
fragile freedom

suicide
because we wait for fate
to favor our song to belong
play today!

Full of It

sitting on the sun-drenched porch, reading,
a squirrel fracas fomented
the overhead tree branch
don't know how squabbles get incited
shook the limbs and leaves with frenzy
seven or eight incensed rodents were squeaking
and chasing after the little
then the little bites the bigger the drama
from a squirrel infraction
the uproar called to mind
there's often much carrying on
about a whole lot of zip, full of sound
and fury
just watch cnn fox nbc abc cbs etc

A Name

the sound of a name
the true measure of wealth
the fame or the shame
the mirror of the self
swelling with acclaim
reputational frame
just one can be blamed
for whatever became
of a name

Threading The Dawn

My self in esse is more
Felt than a weather eye
Fluid as the sea
Tween shores of this earth cup.

Treading the gelid dawn
Riding every trough and rise
The timber of the rib cage
Buoy the ship above the flood.

Albatross of the sky
The forecaster of the day ?
Plunges to the deck
To hang around the neck.

Nimble as a flute
Aerobatic in the air;
A lunar landing swoon
May daze a sailor mooned.

But the adroit sea captain
Shuns nymph siren songs
Linked to starboard and port
To reach the farther shore.

Rocking Africa

A green mamba coiled around a branch
hanging in my front yard,
A sour-smelling hog rooting
just out my front door
A monitor lizard, like a caiman
sunbathing on my bedroom windowsill,
I caught it fast as lightning
and wore it alive like a stole.

I saw green vervet monkeys
swing in the banyan trees near my house
I met scientists who studied them
for their HIV-like viruses
I heard the big bird hornbill croaking
cussing like a sailor
from the ancient Mama Matere tree
I sat gazing at the bathwater Indian ocean
waves steaming off the Mombasa sand.

Overgrown forests,
the crocs and hippo submarines
eying me from Kisumu's Lake Victoria
and elephant-trodden mountain hills
& the savanna safari sights
I remember the lion paws on the Land Rover
bonnet
the big cat staring me in the eye

behind the windscreen glass
his female harem's maws,
carmine from a warthog carcass.

I remember Ramadan at night
on the Swahili streets, the smell
of meat kebabs roasting on wooden sticks
in the heavy tropical air
filled with greetings and guffaws.

I loved riding the EAR train
from Nairobi to the coast
the smells and sights of a diverse world
rocking in my coach.

The Joy of the Cherry Brook Childhood

joy
the fountain of the breast
of childhood with no dam

sunrise after
and dark earlier
back to school in a few days

cherry brook tree
swim on the back
floating in pond water
the bites of horse and deer flies

run up a clover covered hill
king of the grassy green mountain

blue crested kingfishers skim lake
crowds of birds, ducks, geese
snapping turtle snaps at stick
dad kills for soup

the lake next to dark forest trees
weaves of vines
kelly the cat purrs for a belly scratch
the tortoiseshell fisher cat

sun-browned
half-pint boy sits on the dock

holds a bamboo pole with
tangled strings, hands to dad
fixed
under ultraviolet
throws a bob in the lake

dark clouds hang lowering the sky
flash and the claps count
by the thousandths

sprawling green yard decked
with clover and dandelion flowers
mom's lady slipper orchids
purple mouths

a barn refurbished into the red house
dad built
water slide rides into the lake

the fowl-mouthed man next door
pats gigi, their orange collie
the bricklayer froths expletives

his daughters, the three girls next door
crowd of neighbors for a weenie roast
dixie cups of kool-aid
cans of shlitz beer

september to october
cold winds blow
baseball into football

the barn house roof with chimney
a curling sleeve of smoke

Freeze Frames

saw bio mother at the table
me, the baby with eyes of children

the head recording the film
of the camera captured world freezing

the frames of her teardrop wetted face
points the road to Fosterhood

Handed over to a new home by a midwife
placement agent the road to

A deep water lake full of mallards
nearby a river for camp tubing

Family dinner nights, view the Zenith
tv trays, mom's burgers, canned chili beans

The middle title I picked after the rabbit
but mom baptizes the apostle

Hide and seek on eight acres of rural
land, hide in hedges, knuckle my brother

Legs run the forest at night, the hoot of
the owl with clicking eyes like mine

Catching Luckystars

I grew up in a farming village
of dirt roads and the smell of cut hay,
barnyard odors of fertilizer.

Father rebuilt a barn into a farmhouse,
oak milking stanchions lined the kitchen hall
to the cherry wood table and lathe-peg chairs,
the dinner table set those two boys
ate breakfast, lunch, and dinner
from mom's gas-stove cooking.

The fireplace hearth made of quarry stones
lilt-scented the family room with smoke
from winter chimney fires. The brass
poker tools stood next to the metal log holder
stacked with newly hewn pine wood.

The homestead spanned eight acres
of a fish-stocked lake,
tall grass to mow, and grapevine-hung
forests. Dad called it "Cherry Brook."

This, the wild playground for two
little stepchild lads. The tubular swing set
with chain-hung swings, the monkey bars
for monkey shines, hanging upside-down

bar behind the knees,
and pull-up muscle building.

Catching bugs
in jars, frogs in tin pails, and tail-whoopings
from mom and dad some days,
I count those luckystars
and remember.

Stilled the Water

i witnessed a friend gulp his last
air, machine tube mask, plug wired,
oscilloscope digital numbers
dwindling throb. The deep reach,
the shallow swallows. My friend's
baby-blues now gray milk dud stare, then
another slack face mask, the choking
gag, the gone, then I saw nobody. Just
a flank of worm meat. A nurse entered,
felt the jugular and announced the TOD,
the bell tolled, ringing in the siesta
from his hellish mortal coil,
the hand in the Hand.

Resurrection Spring

sans the white blowing cold sky
sans the creaking trees stand like gray octogenarians
sans icicles arm the eaves like impaling fangs
wind chill minus zero nostril juice cracks
sans furnaces grumble money out of registers

now the trees dotted with buds
now robin chirping window knocking
now sun blue warm Easter egg powder hues
now resurrection Spring

Von Doos Gazooks Ape

Von Doos Gazooks Ape
sat upright on the bed
with her triathlon medals
around his neck
fifty years old, if a day

the stuffed animal of a little blonde
farm girl from rural
Ohio, Velveteen
Von Doos is charcoal black
with most of his fuzz loved off
but still adored by that child
now residing in the vintage
sixty year young shell

her heart
every bit as childlike as the day
she first held Gazooks as her
Christmas gift at ten
(and came up with his colorful title)

I introduced to
the balding Ape looked and saw
the object of her love
me falling for this little farm girl
of Latvian hazel eyes

(or lapis lazuli blue
depending on the light)

me the dark brown haired
eagle-eyed rural
boy living and loving her
in my sixty six
gray-headed body

Lapis

Reset me in a blue star sapphire
a star of India
girl
the rumble of nimbus gray

brass drums from the sky lake
travel the asphalt highway
exit to the bumper to bumper cars

I'm on my war horse to see you
to kiss you goodbye

the treasure at Rock Creek
you the measure of my blue
for a month

Triathlon Race

Arms as oak roots, with a bronze of ginger hue
Clad round; rock pads for peck-breasts; the waist, lank.
Thruster quads; knee hinge; and muscled shank—
Two-headed calves, hinge, ankle-foot to crank
By a goggle-eye head swam swell two-point-four queue,
Stand ashore and run, reach bicycle hung, helmet too;
That orange-barreled street, suck air and crank
Suck and crank—,
Tho' as a piston-leg run, up-hill-down, roll swift to rank
And like steel-cable flesh, and the gut-wrenching ride to do—
The hundred-twelve bulging sinew-cycle do.

Drafting, elbows lean into, saddled, bent over at the waist,
In her, all head held to the tip of the bike; lip curls
Hook-hang the bike, in a whirlwind, run wind-laced—
Gassed, see her motor-foot now; wind laced.
Steady pace, don't bonk, she twenty-six-point-two, paced or hurls,
With them—she pads her frowning crushed feet; raced
Ahead, she reads the overhead flag finis-line furls—
With-a-last-burst she's arms-raised under the furls.

My Dad, Sgt Brian G. Hodgkinson

"be alert, they're on the move,"
the squawk box chirps, "eyes peeled!"
through the fire of the flashing flak,
his Supermarine drones on.

It's October 27th, 1941
involved in the fray that must be won.
Hunted by the feral hound unknown,
on the blasts of fate, thrown.

Some say the spitfire swayed the war.
Nimble & quick, the fighter was;
the winged Rolls of British lore,
the legend fans still adore.

There and then, his plane is out flanked.
The Messerschmidt roared up and banked;
talons raked the cockpit's shell,
jolting slammed against his skull.

The panel instruments all went insane,
drenched in fuel & him aflame
ejected how? He can never explain,
aloft, on fire, outside of the plane.

dangling on chute straps, flesh charred & seared;
the vulture returned as his vision cleared.

Coming right at him. Why? He knows.
He drew the last before he goes.

Somehow managed his trademark smile;
he'd make his exit dressed in style,
saluted the pilot in midair -
the ace snapped it back but only could stare.

6-foot-6 soldier, with clothing afire
harnessed & torn, torched & bleeding,
but for a miracle - an aerial pyre,
the rain clouds quenched him, interceding.

He swooned, covered with blood and vomit,
passed through the sky, a smoldering comet.
Descended on Dunkirk, the Nazis were waiting
four years the prisoner of their hate crimes

exactly 60 years later, fading, he lay
still, shrapnel filled from the earlier day,
hemorrhaging within, the doctors all went
the last words as he crashed,
"...a hell of a predicament...."

but as he dropped down
through the murky unknown,
was caught up with laughter
that mirrored his own.
loved ones were waiting
to comfort him home.

Made in the USA
Monee, IL
23 August 2023